info buzz

Hinduism

Izzi Howell

W

FRANKLIN WATTS

LONDON•SYDNEY

Franklin Watts
First published in Great Britain in 2018 by The Watts Publishing Group
Copyright © The Watts Publishing Group, 2018

Produced for Franklin Watts by
White-Thomson Publishing Ltd
www.wtpub.co.uk

ISBN: 978 1 4451 5964 5
10 9 8 7 6 5 4 3 2 1

Credits
Series Editor: Izzi Howell
Series Designer: Rocket Design (East Anglia) Ltd
Designer: Clare Nicholas
Literacy Consultant: Kate Ruttle

The publisher would like to thank the following for permission to reproduce their pictures: Alamy: ART Collection 6, Nisarg Lakhmani 18, Vehbi Koca 21; Getty: SoumenNath cover and 16b, Bartosz Hadyniak 7, Phillipe Lissac 14r, anshu18 16t, Visage 17b; Shutterstock: espies title page and 13, szefei 4, Dipak Shelare 5l, Marina Shanti 5r, I Wei Huang 8, eFesenko 9, CHEN WS 10, neelsky 11, JOAT 12, szefei 14l, Milind Arvind Ketkar 15, highviews 17t, Kertu 19, Tatiana53 20t, Alexander Mazurkevich 20b.

Every attempt has been made to clear copyright. Should there be any inadvertent omission please apply to the publisher for rectification.

Printed in China

Franklin Watts
An imprint of
Hachette Children's Group
Part of The Watts Publishing Group
Carmelite House
50 Victoria Embankment
London EC4Y 0DZ

An Hachette UK Company
www.hachette.co.uk
www.franklinwatts.co.uk

All words in **bold** appear in the glossary on page 23.

Contents

What is Hinduism?

People who are Hindus pray to gods and goddesses. They **worship** at home and in a mandir.

▲ This Hindu family is celebrating the Divali festival at home (see page 16).

Hindus believe in one **powerful** God who can look like different gods and goddesses.

▲ Ganesha is a Hindu god with the head of an elephant.

◄ Lakshmi is a Hindu goddess with four arms.

Hindu books

There are many Hindu books. They tell stories about the gods and goddesses.

▼ In one story, the god Vishnu turns into a fish. Then, he fights an evil monster.

Vishnu

The books also explain how to be a good Hindu. Hindus believe that you should be kind to people and animals.

▼ Cows are important animals for Hindus.

Why should we be kind to animals?

The mandir

Hindus go to a mandir to worship.
Some Hindus visit the mandir every day.

This mandir
is in London.
It has lots of
decorations. ▶

Inside the mandir, there are statues of gods and goddesses. **Priests** look after the mandir.

▲ Some mandirs have colourful painted walls.

Do you live near a mandir? Where is it?

Worship

Hindus ring a bell when they enter the mandir. The sound tells the gods they have arrived.

▲ Hindus pray in front of the statues. They thank the gods and ask them for help.

Hindus bring flowers and food to the mandir as presents for the gods and goddesses.

▲ Priests put the presents in front of the statues.

At home

Hindus make a special place to pray in their house. This is called a **shrine**.

▲ These candles and flowers are presents for the god Ganesha.

Hindus often worship together with their families at home.

▼ This Hindu family is praying together at home.

What do you do with your family at home?

A Hindu life

Hindus celebrate special moments during their lives.

▲ They have a ceremony to give a new baby his or her name.

Little girls have their ears pierced in a Hindu ceremony. ▶

Hindus get married in a mandir. In a Hindu wedding, the couple say seven prayers.

The bride touches a stone with her foot every time they say a prayer. ▶

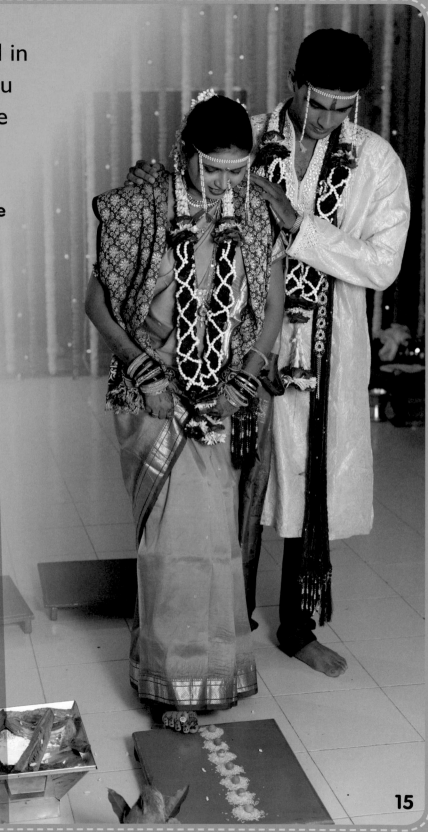

Divali

Divali is the Hindu festival of light. It lasts for five days in October or November. Hindus decorate their homes with **oil lamps**.

A Divali oil lamp

People make patterns with coloured sand at Divali. ▲

Hindus give each other presents for Divali. They eat Indian sweets and other special foods.

Indian sweets are made with milk, nuts and spices. ▶

▼ Hindus often give clothes as Divali presents.

When do you give and receive presents?

Holi

Holi is a spring festival. It celebrates a Hindu story in which a good man wins a fight against an evil king and his sister.

▲ A model of the evil sister is burnt in a bonfire on the night before Holi.

On Holi, people throw coloured **powder** and water at each other. They sing and dance in the street.

▼ Adults and children celebrate Holi together.

Would you like to celebrate Holi? Why or why not?

Around the world

There are many Hindus in India. This is where Hinduism started. The Ganges River in India is very important for Hindus.

India

▼ Hindus swim in the Ganges River.

Today, there are Hindus in many countries around the world. Hindus live on different **continents**, such as Europe, North America and Africa.

▼ **These Hindus are celebrating Divali in London.**

Quiz

Test how much you remember.

Check your answers on page 24.

1 Which god has an elephant's head?

2 What do Hindus do first in a mandir?

3 How many prayers are there in a Hindu wedding?

4 How long does Divali last?

5 In which festival do people throw coloured powder?

6 Where did Hinduism start?

Glossary

ceremony – a special event

continent – a large area of land that is split into different countries

evil – very bad

oil lamp – a lamp which burns oil to make light

powder – a dry substance made of many small bits

powerful – describes someone who is control and can do lots of things

priest – someone who works in a mandir

shrine – a special place to pray. It might have a picture or a small statue to remind people who they are praying to.

worship – pray or do something special to show that you think a god is important

Index

Answers:

1: Ganesha; 2: Ring a bell; 3: Seven; 4: Five days; 5: Holi; 6: India

Teaching notes:

Children who are reading Bookband Gold or above should be able to enjoy this book with some independence. Other children will need more support.

Before you share the book:

- Are any of the children in your class Hindus? Can they tell you about their experiences and understanding?
- Talk together about the religions of other children. What is the same/what is different from Hindu children's experiences?

While you share the book:

- Help children to read some of the more unfamiliar words and concepts.

- Talk about the questions. Encourage children of different faiths and no faith to share their own answers.
- Talk about the pictures. Help children to identify who or what the captions refer to: Where are the statues (p10)? Who is the priest (p11)? Where is the stone (p15)? Where are the lamps (p16)? Although the vocabulary should be familiar, the context may not be.

After you have shared the book:

- Find out more about other Hindu gods and goddesses. What do people pray to them about?
- Arrange to take the children to visit a mandir. Ask them to look for things mentioned or shown in the book.
- Work through the free activity sheets from our Teacher Zone at www.hachettechildrens.co.uk

Series Contents Lists

Religion

Christianity

978 1 4451 5962 1

What is Christianity?
The Bible
Going to church
Communion
Praying
A Christian life
Christmas
Easter
Around the world

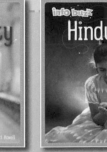
Hinduism

978 1 4451 5964 5

What is Hinduism?
Hindu books
The mandir
Worship
At home
A Hindu life
Divali
Holi
Around the world

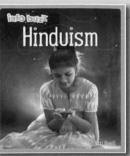
Islam

978 1 4451 5

What is Is
The Qur
The mos
Prayir
Cloth
A Muslir
Ramac
Eid al
Around th

History

Neil Armstrong

978 1 4451 5948 5

Queen Elizabeth II

978 1 4451 5886 0

Queen Vi

978 1 445

Countries

Argentina 978 1 4451 5958 4
India 978 1 4451 5960 7
Japan 978 1 4451 5956 0
The United Kingdom 978 1 4451 5954 6

FRANKLIN WATTS